<u>I pray « Ré » when you pray « Râ »</u>

<u>By Abdallah Idouakrim</u>
<u>English version</u>
<u>Copyright 2020</u>

The scriptures tech us that pharaoh is dead : wrong.
The pyramid is a message of mathematical rules and mine is that the « Great Mute » towards me is nothing compares to this madness ; 99 % / 1 %
The financial crises caused by tax havens and their floating capital have even fined governements that is to say the People (the 99 % who pay taxes) when it was necessary to bail out the banks with public funds.
History teaches us that the people have already awakened in the past at the time when the common man wanted to be entitled as pharaoh to eternity by mummification.
In return, people had to work their whole lives for the embalming ceremony, the funeral papyrus and the temple blessing ! ! !
A bit like at present, we go into debt for the credit of our house.
Our children should not ber born with a debt but rathe with an annuity.

On earth, we are all like « garimpeiros » with more or less enviable statutes which fuel the fire of Hell for the majority and of Paradise for these one per cent.

foreword:
victim of a ratonnade in 1988 in the barracks and on waking up; I was provoked by Sergeant Blocke and hit the next moment by a conscript in the back of the head.
The shock resulted in post-traumatic amnesia for over 30 years.
Having been made to look like the assailant it was not in the infirmary but in the hole that I had a near-death experience.

My travel book where I had recorded impressions being lost, I must try to put together all the pieces of a time puzzle which dates back to my military service and continues in fuzzy times (part of which has been erased by the fog of time and especially drugs).
The heroes of the barracks were for the most part veterans of neo-colonial conflicts and even the doctors who had brutalized me for years: 14 years later their names are still

familiar to me: I quote Commandant Papeeta and Colonel Moutet .

Papeeta had served in Lebanon where he had witnessed the attack which had lengthened eighty-eight French soldiers. This psychiatrist could only hate the Arabs.

At the time, I was stupid not to accept military discipline. "296th day without accident" announced the sign at the entrance to Camp des Garrigues "3rd Regiment of Piedmont Infantry" in Nîmes and yet, each arrival in the blue had its own nightly attempt at suicide. The most unbearable was to realize that a blue man who had tried to end his life had only been taken care of by a roommate who had discovered him lying on the ground when he wanted to surrender in the toilet. When I asked where the infirmary was, I indicated it to him and, taking into account the fact that I had my B.N.S., I asked him to accompany me to see his roommate. When I got there, I was amazed to find that none of the roommates had risen. They seemed rather bothered by the light and turned to present their backs to us. I insulted them because in another situation, that of an armed conflict for example, how could the injured be rescued.

The situation will eventually deteriorate. I was psychotizing too much. I know that this term does not exist in the language of Voltaire, It was coined by the Military. One day, Warrant Officer "Bernede" tries to surprise me in my company retreat office. Seeing his shadow under the door, I decided to water the sprinkler by carrying a truck tire changer on my shoulder which made me quite impressive. Without knowing that I was going to surprise an officer, I suddenly opened the door. How did you know

I was there? he told me. Your Shadow, my adjutant, I replied!

I had just called the B at the bottom of the army to a superior. What we learn from the first field trip. (the "O" from FOMBEC) i From that day on, he never stopped tracking me. The worst thing is that for a given lesson and badly accepted, it endangered the life of Corporal Barbet as well as that of about thirty people as well as civilians and myself of course. It's a little later that Warrant Officer Bernede will give me a truck with a brake problem. When I leave the Camp, I ask them, they do not respond. The terror can be seen on the face of poor Corporal Barbet, who has turned green with fear. However, I was cowardly in agreeing not to see the General to explain my actions. I happened to bathe in the middle of January in the pond in front of the offices of the Kommandantur. Captain "Cendre" who comes to my memory like the phoenix harassed me along the length of my hair to the point that I shaved my head; I was accused of reactionary. I'll end up hitting a hired sergeant who had insulted me; I then found myself in isolation. It should be noted that the model letter written by a Captain, I kept it after making a scene in which I burned a blank sheet to make it appear as the model. I kept her until the Military Hospital to entrust her to someone on whom I let all my hopes for justice rest.

But before, I was in solitary confinement and the guys in my cell were kind enough to lend me their music station. In light clothing, I face the air currents that cross my only cell and go on a hunger strike. I'll even have a bizarre experience: Did I come close to death? One day, I feel "my mind" detach from my body, hovering for a moment to return to it the next moment. They ended up making me crack. The army, it was not for me when I was offered to return to the School of Reserve Officer, me, I preferred the Overseas in V.S.Lii. The letter in which I requested this assignment was to go unanswered. However, there were not only bad moments. For example, this gathering of the Saudis with their darboukas, the Zoreilles which echoed the Antillean singer, the soldier Tancré or the meeting with GI'siii. Chief Warrant Officer Prestat was more human, a former train officer in Morocco, he entrusted me with administrative tasks rather than mind-numbing work, but above all he allowed me to reread a book I had read in my father's business : " The Green March ". The only grade I will take in the military will be P 5. I will end up being sent to a civilian hospital after a muscular administration of vials that had at one time made me as apathetic as a sloth (the animal).

I will come out some time later and decided to "turn the page" by stopping all medication. I would realize at my expense that these treatments would become "long-term" and that I had made the mistake of accepting these "legal drugs" from the start. Years (ten) will follow from collapse to stability and vice versa. Periods when I stop taking all of the Bob's Peace Pipe. Shortly after the keel, I return to the neighborhood, which is not very proud to have a considerable amount of medication which takes all of my life meaningless. It was at this time that my brother-in-law intervened again: "the doctor" He decided to take me under his wing while he was working at the CHS de Montfavet very close to Avignon. I will be his personal driver and a very poor companion. The frog who complains about the "foul pool" in which it bathed will want to know everything about the Ocean that it has hitherto ignored. His illness is an ocean of questions even for those seeking to cure it. My salvation, at a time when I realize that I have great doubts will be going to Brazil. "Seek knowledge even in China"

The day before my twenty-one year, I prepare a box on which I write on one side Lyon and on the other Paris: I will hitchhike. After greeting my doctor who is accompanying me to the highway tollbooth, I present motorists my sign on the Lyon side. I will reach Orly airport at an average speed of 80 km / h. Arrival at the airport will take place at night; I have to pass it in the terminal. In the morning, I board a DC 10 which will make its first ParisFortaleza (Ceara) connection. It was a flight organized by El Condor, the specialist in Latin America. On the plane, I am taken for a Brazilian by the hostesses with whom I joke by thanking them for having thought of my birthday. The arrival in Fortaleza will be about eight hours later, I exult and I am afraid when I arrive. I rejoice because the official welcome is great (an orchestra awaits us with pretty girls who were apparently trying to target their future companion for a moment or more if affinities) but I am starting to worry about the fact that this traveling with a backpack is for me a first and especially that I have heard a lot about insecurity in Brazil. By the way, my only defense taken away from France is a tear gas bomb which will be of some use to me later. The first evening, I leave the hotel with large, newly changed tickets. It will impress a piranha who will hang on momentarily to my t-shirt to the point of tearing it. Despite the pleasant moments spent together, I will tell him that I am "macho" like a South American. This piranha had previously lost me in the city by making me take several buses to introduce myself to a family of her friend in a popular district which reminded me of certain places in Morocco.

On the edge of the beach, there is a certain agitation sprinkled with caipirinha and music. The eletrico trio is already there. The Fortaleza Carnival is not as grand as that of other cities like Rio or Salvador but presents a higher proportion of young women than in the cities of the South which attract the majority of men looking for a job: This confession was made to me by an Indian tourist who apparently knew the subject well. I'll even experience it by being invited by two young Brazilian girls simultaneously. Evening comes and I prepare for the hotel by passing my Senegalese gandoura which obviously has an effect. In general jubilation I meet the "filheus of Allah" and dance throughout the night, stopping from time to time to quench my thirst. New bond at a time. Towards the middle of the night, the BOMBEIROS water us with their fire hose: "Por aqui Manuel" I shout in order to get refreshed. The eletrico trio's orchestra will go so far as to offer the intro to a romantic song decried by the crowd who are only looking for wild rhythms. After a nap on the edge of the hotel swimming pool, I got second-degree burns. Believing that I had a hard skin, I will realize that even under the parasol we tan. At the pharmacy, I hear "Sol de Ceara". On the way to Bélem, my next town where I plan to embark for Manaus, I will meet a pretty Indian half-breed. It is very difficult not to sympathize with people when you are forced to cohabit for a long time in the buses which take several days to reach the different destinations. Bitter observation that to see charred corpses of trees that must have exceeded several tens of meters. As an African African, I have no lessons to teach the Brazilians. The destruction of French or Moroccan forests is the most telling example.

But we are at the time when STING sings the beauty of this dying forest to us. Arrival in Belém will take place in the evening: I plan to go by river to Manaus but my adventures will lead me to deviate from my course. In fact, looking for a place where we can listen to Bahian music, I meet a group of three Brazilians who recommend a dance bar

In the meantime, I've gotten into the habit of changing my big notes for small change to blend in with the crowd. My friends pay in turn for their tours and go so far as to introduce me to one of their friends with whom I sympathize. After a long time that makes me think that I have joined this group, I decide to take the air with my new friend. At the port, we take a snack and try to isolate ourselves. It is then that I will realize how much my new friend cared for me when she told me that her knowledge that came to us was dangerous. Did she appreciate me in such a short time? I prepare my gas bomb and when he arrives at my height with the intention of appropriating my money, I summon him to leave me alone.

There follows a slight brawl in which I spray it with a tear gas. I will give way by abandoning my new friend who was still one of their acquaintances. After a chase, I arrived at the gate of my hotel, panicked. The next day, I'm a little ashamed to admit it, I was still scared. It will only be in the afternoon that I will venture out to take the first taxi to the station and no longer to the pier near the famous "Ver O Peso" market. Having a very long wait at the station, I decide to visit a park whose name I no longer remember, which will be my only getaway in the Amazon jungle. I'll see pacas, birds like macaws or toucans and a manatee. It will also be my only encounter with the problem of the Amazon Indians.

Direction "Rio de Janeiro": I still found a new weapon that will comfort me in the future. Indeed, I had lost my tear gas bomb in the brawl in Belém, so I replaced it with a large craft machete that I bought ten dollars. This machete will reassure me later during my journey of several thousand kilometers in this fantastic country. The sculptures and the snake skin of the scabbard make it a very nice gift that I will leave on my return to my older brother. The arrival in Rio de Janeiro will take place at night after a journey of more than three thousand kilometers which will have allowed me to sympathize with locals. The fact remains that I am once again seized by a feeling of insecurity arriving at the station. I would take the first bus in the direction of "Casa do studente" de Botafogo, a place recommended by the backpacker's guide. I am reassured to find a free room there and impatient to reach the top of the Corcovado. It will not be until the next day that I will begin its ascent of course thanks to the little train that leaves from Cosme Velho.

At the top, the view is magnificent: the drop of more than 700 meters makes a great impression. But during my little journey from Cosimo Velho to Christ on the Cross, I crossed a wooded park on the slopes. I would then like to go there on foot. What I had to do the next day. Back to Cosme Velho, I ask a guard from a rather affluent home for directions. He then politely showed me the path I should follow. I borrow it and end up in a pretty forest which I believe was a natural park. Halfway there, I find myself at the edge of a favela. I have to hide my camera and especially my speech which would betray me. "Tudo bom?" Tudo bem! I replied to some who crossed my path. It was only after my return that the guard of the villa announced that I was coming from afar. According to him and a week before, the favelados had killed a person who had dared to follow the path I had taken.

During my stay in Rio, I behaved a bit like a "Pivete", that is to say, a young man on the street. Besides, one day when I was waiting for the bus barefoot of course, I was quickly checked by the police who searched me the only place where I could hide some weapon; my parts. The bus, taken free of charge and from where you have to jump on the road when the stop is not requested by someone who has paid for it, takes us to "Barra de Tijuca", the beach in vogue at that time. I say "we" because at the hostel, I sympathized with a Peruvian and a Chilean who will be temporary adventurers. On the beach, the rollers are quite important and we surf my friends and I without a board, that is to say that we swim towards the coast when approaching a big wave and that we let ourselves be towed. Sometimes it pulls us for a few seconds and can break our back when caught in a roll. In the evening, on the avenue that borders the beach of "Copacabana", we meet an authentic garimpeiro who tells us about his adventures in the Amazon rainforest. After many adventures and the theft of my "Reebok", I decide to join the city where is the airport from where I will embark to join France: On the way for Salvador de Bahia. In the bus that takes me there, I am seduced by "Bettina", a Uruguayan who was traveling with one of her friends..

The forty-eight hour trip will allow us to sympathize and plan our visits to Salvador because I joined them. Hosted one night by another traveler, we decide to go to Ilha de Mare. This island is only accessible through smugglers who, for a nominal fee, take you on their boats. During the crossing of a few minutes, I appreciate the setting and the idyllic conditions. When we get to the island, we go to the only hotel owner who runs a few huts and a restaurant. After renting our drop-off point, we bathe in the small beach which puts us in contact with the inhabitants of the nearby big city. In fact this island is a resort for some inhabitants of Salvador. This is where we will meet "Madre Heloisa" and her little family. We are invited to taste mangoes and lobster. I am joking when I say that I was the son of "Iemandja" a goddess of the Brazilian pantheon because I was born on February 2, the day on which she is celebrated. So will start a friendship with this family who will invite us to their house on the outskirts of Salvador. But in the meantime, we set out to discover the island by spotting monkeys and more easily spiders. On the coast, there is another restaurant on stilts where we were invited by an Salvadoran who took care of the animation on this place. Result of the races, I will be the only one to eat the "feijoada" this famous Brazilian dish because arrived on his boat, a distinguished guest: the singer "Milton Nascimento" who still had a big head and locks. Autographs will only be signed after lunch; Bettina was disgusted and I didn't care.

During a trip in town, I am fascinated by the comrade of a backpacker who is nothing other than a marmoset; I decided to buy it from him. And the renamed "Tio" named after a brand of rice. This marmoset that I could get through customs and which will become my companion after my return to the "foul pond". At the bus stop, there is someone demonstrating with an electric gymnot, this eel capable of lighting the bulb which he cleverly connected with electric wire. Praia do forte, next destination. On this beach, we will visit the sea turtle farm of the World Wildlife Fund and we will see tropical fish while swimming in the lagoon. Arembepe, the artists' beach: The beaches are huge and sometimes almost deserted, you would think you were Robinson Crusoe. After choosing where to spend the night, I advise my friends to bury the backpacks and sleep on them in case a marauder tries to steal them from us.

The feeling of change of scenery is intense and the setting romantic. Oddly enough, Bettina's only memory will be to shake hands tenderly during this interminable night because it was awake. The next day, I try in vain to bring back a coconut which will finally be offered to us by a couple who had hitchhiked us. Tio jumps on my hand which contained the fruit and begins to devour the object of his lust. And then, the return to Salvador is essential. We want to join the Family of Madre Heloisa. I would receive as a gift a book of poems illustrated by the son Claudio and whose title was "Passaro silente" (the silent bird). He had just fallen not from the nest but into the hands of a "passaro silente" who kept everything inside him; did i have a look or attitude that signified the hardships i had endured? The message I would like to send to Bettina, Madre Heloisa, Claudio is that the bird finally sings! They had planted a seed on a ground which asked only to make it germinate. Seeing that I had accomplished myself very well on this trip, being careful not to fall into the tourist traps, I felt that I would start again in another direction. I discovered Capoheira there long before it was publicized in France and sipped whole cans of guarana, this drink whose plant extracts are produced from an indigenous essence. The arrival in Roissy but especially the crossing of Paris will make me discover how happy I was there: the Parisians with their blinders and the empty face surprised me because in other latitudes but with a state of destitution more important the Brazilians display a smile. The return to Montpellier will be hitchhiking again and with the same average speed as on the outward journey. I was in a hurry to return to the neighborhood this time with my head held high and full of good memories. Did I want to repair the image of the return from my military service which had been rather a rout?

The fact remains that I did not return to my brother-in-law's, determined to keep certain principles that he had instilled in me and to apply them in my life. There followed a period when I tried to occupy my moments of idleness by going to see a large number of films especially foreign to the cinema. However, my newspaper readings always put the Palestinian problem back on the carpet. I returned to sport and I can boast of being in good physical condition. After having cogitated quite often, then the idea of a march towards the Holy Land takes shape in my mind. At that time, an Algerian Djamel went around the world as a marathon runner.

His example prompts me to consider an exploit coupled with a symbolic. Join the youth intifada but above all be present as a journalist and not as a terrorist. Before, I have to go there: but how? I then plan to leave Morocco and cross all of North Africa on horseback in a first project. This solution will not be adopted. Having also read that all clothing in the colors of the Palestinian flag was prohibited by the Hebrew state, I decided to play the provocation by making a tricolor sweatshirt (green, black and white): Red could only be added by balls that would make injury or death illegal under Israeli law. So I improvise as a fashion designer. The days go by but are not alike except for the news which always announces more deaths. So I became impatient to leave but I had to work before. After two months of work in a locksmith's shop, I have about five thousand francs in front of me which will allow me to reach the first stage of my new journey: Morocco and beyond the Unknown. I have two passports in my pocket: French and Moroccan. On that of France, I had applied for the Egyptian visa. That of Morocco would allow me to cross the Greater Maghreb to Libya.

The day of my departure, the omens are good with an eclipse supposed to prove it. In my luggage, there is a Zenith brand camera with its fairly powerful zoom lens and a large number of film, everything for the perfect reporter; I also took my almost finished nationalist sweater. I would entrust it to a Moroccan seamstress for the finishing touches. I also forgot several geographic maps (North Africa, India, China and Israel). Arrived in Rabat, I visit the family. From the start, I am talking about my future adventure which greatly surprises those around me as much as the news from the front is rather disturbing.

My cousin will accompany me to the seamstress and will go as far as being photographed with my unfinished "flag". I will still have the support of the majority of young people to whom I revealed "my secret".

Many of them would even have accompanied me if they could have had two passports like me. It is the ideal place to visit the various diplomatic representations with a view to the granting of a visa; it will ultimately be that of Egypt that I will obtain for a period of three months. I then take the direction of Marrakech with my father. We are going to our adored aunt. The reaction of the young people around my cousins is also unanimous: We are with you. Besides, Hafiz, the blacksmith will even sharpen a souvenir dagger bought earlier in the souk. He will also engrave his initials there. I felt puffed up with pride at being able to make this somewhat hazardous journey; my knowledge of Arabic being only elementary. It was from Marrakech that I was thinking of starting my journey but before I wanted to go back to basics in the Anti-Atlas. Tamellakoute is a village near Taliouine where my father was born and raised..
This place is quite far from everything and the locals cling to a land a little too hard to cultivate, not to say ungrateful. We are in August and the village is preparing to celebrate "Rma sidi Youssef Bnou Ali". I would attend this event even if my head was elsewhere. To return to Tamellakoute, it should be noted that he is part of the "Oun Zine" tribe: My tribe. This village is only accessible after several hours spent avoiding the big stones of the track and the streets

have no name. This land is the kingdom of scorpions, snakes and some partridges. I was going to forget the stray dogs reminiscent of Australian dingoes. It's the sub-desert steppe. This place fascinated me when I was young because it reminded me of a timeless place. In my youth, we lit up with the gas lamp, we milked the cow by hand and above all we walked on donkey or mule. Later, the generator sets with their deafening din appeared, as did the tractors. It should be recalled that the RTM (Radio Television Marocaine) was not received there but had been replaced by satellite kits. After a week, I decide to leave the village to meet an uncle in Marrakech. I had agreed on an appointment to buy a mount at the souk. After careful consideration, I give up the idea of taking as a companion in misfortune a horse that I will not be sure I can feed well but also quench my thirst especially since I plan to follow the southern edge of the Atlas from Algeria and beyond the edge of the desert. The idea of doing this bike trip is given to me but I don't like it too much; symbolically the image is less beautiful than that of a beautiful horse. It is October and the nights are getting cooler. My cousin will accompany me to a cycle seller where I will stock up on tires, tire changers, patches; in short, enough to be able to repair any breakdowns on the way.

At that time, I feel that my presence drags a bit on the current news: I must leave quickly enough as my trip must take a long time. My aunt will bake anise-based cookies on two baking sheets that my cousin will take to the oven. At that moment, I feel that it is practically impossible to go back even if the situation "there" has deteriorated.

To listen to the news, I bought myself a small radio station to follow them on Radio France Internationale. It's a beautiful morning when I decide to leave without trying to say goodbye to my father lest he try to hold me back. My cousin, this sportsman, will go as far as accompanying me running about twenty kilometers out of Marrakech. After greeting him, I found myself alone on my brand new bike. The first stage takes me to Kelaa-des-Sraghna, about a hundred kilometers further. Morale is good enough, the condition too. The road I take follows the northern edge of the Atlas in a pretty green landscape. It's a first for me, traveling alone (without my parents) in Morocco. I will arrive in the evening, at the home of a family friend whose address I had received from my cousins. It should be noted that I surprised him with my paraphernalia. Surprised, we were surprised by a thunderstorm that had flooded the entire interior courtyard of the house.

After a meal and the answer to the questions he was asking about the direction of this expedition, I went to bed slightly tired. After an early breakfast, I decided to hit the road, setting myself as the second stop in the town of Béni-Mellal. The road is always pleasant and the hundred kilometers that separated me from the stopover town is swallowed in a day. So I arrived there at the end of the afternoon but not knowing where to sleep I preferred to go beyond the city; and then I got to the Royal Gliding Center where I thought I could spend the night. The ensuing problem was that I had arrested a worker's wife; undertake such a great journey without knowing that you should never talk to a single woman. The constable who stood guard then addressed me, summoning me to follow him into his office. It was then that an interrogation began in which I had to tell him all the places I had visited until then. I'll give him the Hebrew state card and ask him to let me sleep. After several phone calls, he finally offered to rest on the entrance terrace; I was still free. On the third day of my departure, I begin to penetrate a little more the mountain ranges, the landscape is splendid but my legs have more difficulty in advancing my bicycle. Arrived at Zaouïa Cheikh,

I meet the owner of a cafe who was intrigued by the adventurer that I was. He greeted me in his shed (my confidence is total), then showed me the nearby river where I was going refresh me. After a massage with a muscle balm, I took a little nap to wait for the arrival of the coach which would help me cross the endless mountain slopes.

In the afternoon I got up and discussed my plans with this stranger who had offered me hospitality. He himself had ventured to Central Asia and had almost married an Uzbek woman. I then, after the greeting of uses, took the bus for the town of Rich which I would reach during the night.

Upon arrival, I rest near a wall of the small station. I still made a journey of more than three hundred kilometers by bicycle. I decided to join Gourama, a small town where one of my cousins taught, who had urged me to join him during my visit. Fifty kilometers ahead, I'll do it in record time since I'm on the southern slopes of the Atlas. My cousin, his wife and their son are amazed to see me so far from Rabat and always as motivated. I would stay two days to prepare to face this time the great stranger: From now on, I would no longer have a family pied-à-terre and that until Libya where lived an uncle of whom I only had the address coffee where he was supposed to work. I left the third day in the direction of Ksar Es Souk (Errachidia), passing a flood in flood, I program my camera for the souvenir photo. After the ascent of a painful hill, I dominated the southern slope of the Atlas and the plain of Errachidia, moreover, in the descent I had almost taken the shortcut of the precipice because of the centrifugal force. From the station, I was about to reach the Algerian border which had been reopened. I did not know what the customs officers' reaction would be to my view. In the bus that takes me to the border, I meet a Japanese tourist my age: Kazuhiro. We sympathize and decide to make part of our trip together. Now, I have got into the habit of taking my bike as luggage, for which I pay a tax. Kazuhiro talks to me about visiting the Algerian city of Ghardaïa which will be a stage on the journey that we jointly decide on. But before that, we are at the border post on the Moroccan side. We took a room in a small hotel whose boss had an acquaintance in Algeria who would receive us to change our currencies. The next day, Kazuhiro and I crossed the border. I left a guide from Morocco to a customs officer as a gift. At that time, the amount of currency taken by the tourist was noted on the passport. I will have nothing to report since I was on my bike.

On arrival at Aïn Sefra, we are greeted by the money changer who received us at his home. He offered us an exchange rate seven to eight times higher than the official rate. For two hundred French francs, I was able to cross the entire Algerian territory (transport, food and accommodation).

This gentleman even offered us tours around the city but Kazuhiro and I decided to progress towards the Sahara towards the small town of Ghardaïa. Departed at night, we arrive in the early morning on an endless road. During stops, we realize that the djellaba is very useful where there is no bush to hide. In the distance, you can see the flames of the oil installations. Arriving in Ghardaïa, we head to a small hotel in the old town. For two to three days, we will take a stroll in the capital of the Mozabites where we unearth a cafe run by Algerians from France with whom we take coffee or tea from time to time. Kazuhiro, to whom I confided, agreed to follow me on a small portion of the journey. He later called me "crazy" from the Indian city of Puri by sending me a postcard that spoke volumes. Anyway, we take the bus to Touggourt then El Oued. I then understand the fascination exerted by the desert on certain travelers: the sky seems to merge with the earth, such the radiation of the sun is intense. Kazuhiro, he will head to Tunisia and Italy. On the other hand, I keep the direction of the East.

For fear of being worried by customs; I always have a tear gas bomb on me that I will throw in the desert. The Tunisian border is already close but I will have to travel the few kilometers that separate me by bicycle. It was then that in the darkness I heard the barking of stray dogs chasing me; it goes without saying that the pace of my legs has accelerated to the village of Tozeur or Nefta, I have to check on a map. It is widely accepted that any Muslim can request hospitality in the name of God; what I will do when I see a crowd of young people at the entrance to the village. They decide to place me in the garage of a nearby house where a meal is served to me. Attention the taste buds, strongly spicy sensations.

My host will go as far as to attribute to the Moroccans the power to flush out the gold hidden in the houses; the only gold I could think of at that time was the beauty of the young women in the house. The young people who asked me where I was from and where I was going even offered to go to the Club Med in the area, but I preferred to rest. The bus takes me to the next step which makes me see the sea again; during my breaks in the cities I go through, I sometimes phone my sister to tell her where I was. Yesterday in Algeria, today in Tunisia and the next day in Libya. Considering the clichés conveyed by the West on this country, I am not very reassured.

One night, I have a dream in which I witness an air disaster and start to play the reporter while photographing this scene. In my dream, people who come to me take me to task precisely because I photograph the blaze. The fact remains that the next day in the bus that heads me to the border with Libya, the driver kills a man in his path. He will deliver himself to the police station where we were stranded until the arrival of a replacement driver. Because of my dream, I didn't photograph anything ... I'll even be bothered by plainclothes police, at least I think, who approached me and asked me if I was carrying drugs. Even my aunt's cakes were tasted. Curiously, I am hitchhiking by a Libyan who will save me a passage of more than a thousand kilometers; the distance that separated us from Tripoli. The road followed the coast and strangely enough there was no sign at the crossroads. My benefactor having asked me about the direction of my trip, I told him that I wanted to join an uncle in Tripoli. When we arrived he offered to accompany me to a noisy cafe where my uncle was supposed to work. The cafe owner must have believed in a police action and tells us that he did not know my uncle's name. Finally, I give up and spend the night next to my guide: the taxi driver. The next day, I take the direction of Benghazi in a coach where everyone is forced to smoke actively or passively. The bus passes by an air base where it is reminded that taking photos can land you in prison. We cross a steppe landscape with large farms that give the image of a rather peaceful people. In Benghazi, the government keeps traces of the bombing of the Americans as relics and tap water tastes salty. It is in this city that I would get a good price from "my mount". As we approach Egypt, there is one last rampart to cross: "El Selloum" the ladder. At the top, the Libyan border post overlooks the Egyptian desert. A winding road winds over a drop of several hundred meters.

At the Egyptian border post, I present my two passports which arouse the suspicion of a chief customs officer who summons me to his office. I make him understand in a non-explicit Arabic that I wish to return to Egypt: He then begins to write in Arabic a text on my French passport in which he alluded to "Hafiz" the name which was engraved on my dagger. Finally, I can continue my journey in the direction of Alexandria at first and then ultimately towards Cairo whose famous pyramids exert their power of attraction on me.

The arrival in Cairo is by the West road from where we can see the imposing monuments. On the way, we (this time again I sympathized with two Algerians) are directed towards the "Oxford pension" in Talaat-al-Harb Street (the street of the rise of the war) not far from Tahrir square by M. Chamis . For practically the entire duration of our stay, he will come regularly to visit us. I think with hindsight that he had to work for state security. This enigmatic character even borrowed my camera to return it to me after a long wait. As if to impress us, he even took us to a prestigious hotel to attend a show; if I remember correctly it was at Kasr-en-Nil. Shortly after our arrival, we decided to go to the Pyramids in Giza: A good distance from the monuments, we are harassed by a horse owner who will finally offer us a good price for the ride. It is then that will follow a joyful escapade in the desert: The horse that I rode gave its maximum in the race that I ordered him. All the same, he will suddenly stop in front of the refreshment bar probably held by "accomplices" of our owner. Still in the desert bordering the city, we approach a camel driver. Djamel the Algerian proposed to ride a camel rather than a dromedary.

Surprised by the sudden lifting of the beast, he swayed in the air before falling like a sack of potatoes: We exploded with laughter in front of the stage which was badly taken by our comrade who continued to rail against the animal .

Regularly, I happened to go to the banks of the Nile which appeased me enormously. As the New Year approached, I was even thinking of swimming there. One day I will visit the Cairo museum fascinated by the objects of the daily life of the pharaohs and especially by the sarcophagus of All-Ankh-Amon. I even imagined a pharaonic outfit for a 21st century lady. Finally, almost at the end of my goal, I decided to go to a travel agency that Mr. Chamis had told me. I would pay my round trip there for "Al Quds": Jerusalem. I would leave one fine morning, towards the station, without my camera so as not to arouse suspicion about my intentions.

Quickly, I found myself on a ferry crossing the Suez Canal and further on, I was in the Sinai desert. The war which took place there is remembered by the carcasses of tanks which almost twenty years later are wiped out on the course. In the bus, a French Jew takes his place next to me and asks me about my travel intentions; I explain to him that I have set myself the goal of the "Dome of the Rock", the third holiest place in Islam.
But, I think I was quite tense and moved to be so close to my goal separated only by a border post, the last one: Gaza Strip "Rafaa". On the spot, I am surprised to see that I am summoned by the customs officer who keeps my passport while the Jews (who must have come from Eastern Europe) crossed the station to take the coach waiting for them on the other side . Isolated from the group, I realize that the trip ended there: on the pretext that I did not have enough money, I am turned back. In fact, I was not that isolated because I was relegated to the same point as the Palestinians who were awaiting clearance. It was then that I decided to harangue the "Arabs" present by showing them my "unfinished flag" and explaining to them in

immature Arabic that I had come from France to support their Intifada. At the post, the situation became more and more tense because I rubbed myself against the soldiers who, tired of my protest, decided to send a Jew, probably of Moroccan origin, who returned my passport soiled with an "Entry Denied" stamp and told me got on bluntly in a coach that was going in the opposite direction. This refusal, despite my French passport, will disappoint me to the point that I will live thereafter, a descent into Hell. My progress was stopped net and thereafter the situation will deteriorate. Indeed, I find the Oxford pension which I only left for a long day. The residents around me are of various nationalities. Jeff, the Englishman who seems exasperated by the calls of the Muezzin and who expresses his pride with an "I'm a Viking!" "(I'm a Viking) had a traffic in grass. Upon contact, I start smoking again and will follow a period when I begin to lose touch with reality. The arrival of Sandy, a Greek Jew from Australia will make me fall in love with a woman who, when she does not have heroin, is a human foulbrood. I would advance him a fairly large sum which will seal a passing friendship. I would even go so far as to sing to her: I want to die-ve into your Ocean! This sentence takes on the meaning of diving and dying in "its ocean". She will still protect me from her "trap". She kept repeating when I told her my love: Stop harassing me! I didn't understand how she couldn't have feelings but she explained to me that she was married and that her husband was languishing in Egyptian jails.

She even offered me a Star of David which I began to wear. The presence of Sandy who was very feminine, blonde with green eyes, ignited me and I enjoyed accompanying her through the old city of Cairo arm in arm, arm in arm as if I were her husband.

At least that was the impression left to the Egyptians when they saw us. They would surely have harassed her without my presence or that of another man. We were walking the streets of Khan-El – Khalili and I wanted our moments of complicity to end. I was struck down with Love. One fine day Jeff and a few other Englishmen decided to go south. He left his business without a buyer. It was then that the consumers of herbs asked me to take up the torch, which I did without too much hesitation as my finances began to shrink. I was aware of Jeff's contacts: Sudanese who displayed the colors of the rastas and whose activity had to be tolerated by the authorities. So I decided to "dealer" with the blessing of the occupants of the pension who would be my only clients. I would like to remind you that at that time, I was not aware of it, I was a little delusional. The lack of treatment but also the taking of illicit substances (grass and one day even opium) did not help the rest of the events. My trips out of the pension are less numerous, only to go to the neighboring market to buy bananas, cheese and bread. My food will be frugal and rarely the ordinary is improved by the employees of the kitchen of the pension who invite me from time to time to share their poor meal. I forgot that I was also going out to the second underground market, the latter, Sudanese people who sometimes took me long distances through Cairo to stock up on supplies. Sometimes we would go to the other end of town where I would trade budding the equivalent of about a month's salary for an Egyptian in a single transaction. It should be remembered that from time to time, producers of films or advertising came to recruit extras in the pension which allowed us to earn ten Egyptian pounds for the trip. This is how one day I find myself in military uniform in English in a theater where we were asked to watch the scene for the duration of a take. Curiously, the events that I am recalling now after more than a decade or so have ceased to have the emotional charge that would have made me "cry" over lines of writing. Reading is also my refuge at this time, mainly in English. I have, in view of my diplomas, applied for a student card at the University of Cairo plus to benefit from the reductions on the hypothetical return transport to France. Still, I spent long moments at the American library to buy books: "the secret of dreams", "the history of Western philosophy" ... It is in this last book that I will learn that my conduct during military service was strangely reminiscent of that of Socrates almost two thousand years ago. I would even surprise myself one day saying to my sister on the phone that: "diseases are just words! "

My mind is bubbling, I would also write my vision of the news in the form of a poem perhaps to exorcise my fear of possible reprisals which had made me paranoid: The tears of the Jews irrigate the Negev Bloodstroke of the Palestinians Tears of newborns Larvae on the hungry The rest will be lost in my different "moves".

I sometimes go for solace in the El-Azahar mosque but my mind is already too far away. I will regret not having answered in the affirmative to the proposal made by the owner who housed me and who would have employed me as a reception agent. It's also a day when I am very upset that I meet an individual who decides to take me home; I was on the street. My French passport had perished in the flames, that of Morocco was taken hostage by the owner of the pension; I was just a clandestine. I could no longer receive help from France who no longer had an address and, in a burst, I had tried to go to Crete to work there picking oranges. The demand for labor allows some backpackers to rebuild their financial health. Israel also offers some travelers the opportunity to work in a Kibbutz or Moshav while able-bodied men bear arms. To come back to this last return attempt, this is how the events unfolded: I went to a travel agency where I wanted to pay for my passage to the Orange Island. I had the cash and the employee told me that I needed proof of the Change. I brought it back to her an hour later, but she wouldn't let me leave the territory. My voice went up, and then another employee, this one man, came to his rescue. Was I on a list of bans from leaving Egypt? I have thought for a long time. Note that the Israeli-Egyptian peace agreement must stipulate some police cooperation. Besides, the events which will follow will confirm me in this hypothesis. Asphyxiated financially and probably banned from leaving the country, I could only find myself in the Shadow. I'm going to live my Egyptian midnight-express.

I ended up landing in a police station and being taken into custody. My jailer kept insulting us, shouting at us: Kisst-oumkoum! It was for our mothers who surely had nothing to do with the situation.

In front of all the prisoners, he asked me if I wanted to go to Jerusalem and used his service weapon to scare me. Handcuffed against a wall, a friend and I contort to do our business by the window. In fact, the handcuffs were not very useful to me since I managed to remove them; indeed, several months of frugal meals had made me the equivalent of an Ethiopian. Exasperated by the actions of our jailer, I decided to rebel by grabbing him by the collar. I was quickly overpowered by another guard who took me up the stairs to see his superior who decided to send me to another prison. Arrived on the scene, I find myself in a place that would fill up later to the rhythm of the big raids made by the Egyptian police. I realize that there is a real security problem: Part of the Egyptian population has still not "ratified" the peace treaty with Israel. During the night, a wagon of "Abdelhak" arrives which, strangely enough, all had the same first name; they were then directed to I don't know where. After several nights and several roundups, I understood that I had to wait for the Ibad-

Llahv's turn. In the cell, there was a small corner of intimacy where the play of the single bulb lit a section of wall which had probably been sculpted by an artist of the shade undoubtedly remained in the shade. You could distinguish it like a smiley face. After several days, I almost lost track of time, I am directed to a third place in which I would feel a little more heat from the occupants. I would find a tourist from the Bahamas Islands met at the hotel and who, according to the latest news, had taken the road back. But he too was there because he had passed the date of his visa. There were other tourists, mostly foreigners, who received food. I have been invited several times by them surely that they felt pity for me. I easily sympathized with the other detainees but after a while the situation became more and more tense. A westerner kept repeating to me in English: "I want to kill you! "Then the situation will deteriorate a little more. The conflict was latent. One day, exasperated by these threats, I hit him with a big knee that broke his brow bone. The guards will eventually arrive, challenged by the cries and will change my cell. Still in the same place but in a smaller cell where I felt less attacked by the light, I dozed off on the edge of a concrete bench seat. When I woke up, I saw a tattoo in front of me that reminded me of Sandy's. It was actually that of a mysterious man who had come close to me.

In the center of the cell, there were only stones of which I was, in my delirium, the only owner. This place would also fill up with the massive influx of prisoners. My mind continued to wander enormously. Sometimes the guards put us in trucks or couriers to take us to Tahrir Square. It's during one of these outings that I find myself handcuffed passing under a metal object detector that rings. I was in the Israeli diplomatic representation in Cairo: Now that you are there. What will you do ? officials said to me. Other outings allowed me to contact the Moroccan representation where there was a woman who felt sorry for me and offered me a sweater which I will not keep long. I will learn on my return that a Moroccan journalist had interviewed me and that he had written a small article which appeared in a Moroccan daily newspaper; I couldn't tell her that I was only waiting for death. After a while, I was taken to a fourth place: I was going to return to the "stable" that is at least the idea that I had when entering my new cell greeted by a large fresh excrement at the entrance. The floor was made of clay and the walls were several meters long. Above the door, there was a wooden lintel attached to a gate: It was my only opening to the outside. The view was limited by overlooking a viewpoint and a perimeter wall. Regularly, I insulted the guards who were toasting on the watchtower. From time to time, they would point their Kalashnikovs at me. I think the ball must have been too expensive for their miserable balance. Sometimes we were fed, I never knew by whom, but I quickly got into the habit of refusing all foods by throwing away the contents of my plates for animals. Indeed, from time to time passed birds (hoopoes, sparrows ...) who came to eat at the expense of my stomach which remained empty. On the other hand, my body quickly became the domain of a whole fauna of small insects swarming in the cell. One day the latter opens and the guard who was a shouter takes me out into the courtyard. I finally have a little moment of supervised freedom. I will re-enter my cell without first taking a shower. We will have to wait for the next one. The outings in the courtyard were the moments to get to know the other locked up "beasts" including an Islamist who did not stop his complaint. One day, I was questioned by an official who took note of my address, my name and a photo of me with a sign on which he marked a number. I was on file. A little later, "an angel" passes on the roof of my "stable" and removes there a box which blocked the only view that I could have on the sky; he brought "TV" into my cell. Now, I could see the parade of stars, clouds ... It was an unforgettable moment.

From time to time, I received one or two cigarettes that I had learned to appreciate. I even had the opportunity to make fire with the old newspapers of "El Ahram" (the pyramid) to which I was somehow "subscribed". A small drawing even showed a man at the bottom of the mastaba with whom I identified. After a while, I am transferred to a central where I will stay for a while. This is where my father's words come back to me when he told me that I would be eaten by "cats". In this hell lived cats that had become wild again because of the mistreatment and the difficulty they had in obtaining food.

Being closer to animals than to humans, I approached them at the risk of being scarred by those who allowed the Romans to take the Egyptian city of ancient Peluse. This plant spanned three levels and being on the first, I had to wipe sputum from above from time to time.

After a while, I am again transferred to the foreigners' cell where I am warmly welcomed. Maybe I missed them, at least my habit of spraying the walls of the toilets to flush out the insects that were there had accustomed them to a semblance of cleanliness. In the bunk bed cell, the Islamists are shocked. I will try to support them even if I do not realize that I may be more to complain about than they are. Finally, after two months of malnutrition but also lack of treatment, I was taken to Cairo airport by a courier. I will arrive in a room where I feel attacked not by the cleaning staff but more by their cleaning product. I will spend the night in this room before being embarked on an Air France flight early in the morning. At the time, I was still forgetting my family's efforts to track me down. My father used to watch the news regularly from the Moroccan Consulate in Montpellier. Dad, I would like to tell you that you did more than give birth; your obstinacy ended up bringing me back from a dramatic journey. The jailers must have thought that I was simply short of heroin or some other drug addict. In fact, I was very sick. Sick, I am still sick at the time of takeoff and in my delirium I remain a prisoner of Egypt. Besides, I'm still afraid of hearing the laughter of the ironic "Zabt" about my situation. The five-hour flight will be an opportunity to improve the ordinary thanks to the meal tray. I will also be difficult to hold in place: The steward was very busy especially when I did not accept to buckle up and stay in my chair.

On arrival in Paris, I will be the last to leave the aircraft to be handed over to my descent at the Air and Border Police.

Once again I will find myself in a cell previously occupied, strange to say, by a bearded woman, before being transferred by ambulance to Antony's Hospital. There I have a large bedroom which dazzles me with its cleanliness. I will regain strength, food and an injection that will make me hover from the Paris region to the Montpellier hospital in La Honte.

Something to crack the most patient of doctors: Result of this trip, several years of effort on the part of Dr. Deddouche who has invested a lot to help me stabilize. But, I repeat with a little bitterness, this trip was practically necessary for me. Is there a causal link between the disastrous experience in the French army and this journey to the same center of tension as the Near East? I think so. In fact, events in France from the start of the second Intifada show that the Beur community is very much identified with the Palestinian cause. Which comforts me to think that if my trip had been publicized, even sponsored, I would not have been alone to present myself at the border post of "Rafaa". Today, I am thirty-four years old and I have more often "experienced", rather seen, the repression of the Zionist state on the Arabs. I believe that if at present, the city of pilgrimage that is Santiago de Compostela was colonized or even ransacked with bulldozers, tanks, the reaction of the Christian community towards of this aggression would be "a public outcry" then an intervention to restore the Order. As in Jerusalem, "Al Quds" the Order being to restore to Islam, its Holy Places. Must we remember that the Philistines who would have been beaten by King David, were the ancestors of the Palestinians? We should recognize the ancestral rights of this people whose historic existence even the historians wanted us to lose by changing their name. Even national education refutes the contribution of the Arab world to the progress of civilization, it is in PS (Post Scriptum) on a teacher's manual that it is specified that the pilot of Vasco da Gama was an Arab. It was completely by chance that this information was disclosed to me. The intifada returns by thousands the stone that once allowed David the Jew to defeat Goliath the Philistine. It is at this level of the Symbolic that the Palestinian action takes place. The creation of the Zionist state robbed the descendants of Goliath a second time. The diaspora of the Jewish people was initialized by the Romans; it would have been wiser to locate the Zionist state in Sicily, for example.

At a time when the situation between Palestinians and Israelis has deteriorated extremely, I despair for those who live the daily humiliation that God does, to live; getting to work after what Censorship wants to let us see has become the biggest challenge of the day.

The problem for all Muslims is that if we plan to make the pilgrimage of Al Quds, it is vis-à-vis the Israeli administration that we must take the step; visas are therefore allocated to the dropper or not even at all as in my case. However, I had my French passport. The occupied territories will be occupied by the Jewish colonies as long as there is water. The "Sheba Farms" in southern Lebanon remained occupied by the Zionist state. The problem is that in the redistribution of land, the Jews appropriated the most fertile and the best irrigated. Too bad, for the Philistines (Filastin in Arabic) they have only to be more powerful. In the Fertile Crescent, Palestinian peasants lag behind in terms of their water supplies. Land war, water war, war of religions - settling of scores between terrorists because Sharon's behavior in Sabra And Shatila is rather that of a terrorist □ (understand SS). It must be said that, all things considered, the student has surpassed the master. The creation of the State of Israel came at a time when the Arabs had become masters of their own destiny, and above all of their oil wells. Creating "cancer" in the Arab world was therefore a solution to disorganize it. The creation of Israel wanted to try to take control of trade on the eastern shore of the Mediterranean. The confusion caused by the massive arrival of Palestinian refugees in Lebanon and Jordan was to allow the Spartan state to control the workings of trade in this area. What a great billiard demonstration? Finally, I realize that it is difficult to be a single Palestinian of fighting age. My reflection joins that of Darwish in one of these poems. I will always remember: "We threw the grammar and its rules into the fire and started the Combat!

AUBE TO WRITING Or the Sense of Crying

Mr. Idouakrim Abdallah

Nanterre, 21 June 2007

Sos Racism Subject: Application for intervention in proceedings against the State for abusive internment in a military environment

Ma'am, sir, the reason I am contacting you today is to provide you with information on the case in question. My name is IDOUAKRIM Abdallah, born on February 2, 1967 in Montpellier, administrative assistant at the DDASS of the hauts de seine and father of two children. In order to better enlighten you about my past, I am enclosing a copy of my manuscript retracing my career from my military service to my commitment to the Palestinian cause. Please note, Madam, Sir, that I doubt the relevance of the military medical file that I could only know from 2002 (law allowing the communication of medical data). Indeed, its reference to the school in Algiers to explain a fatigue due to the punishment of isolation that I suffered in barracks with hunger strike, seems to me implausible. Colonialist and degrading vision of the Arab populations judged as primitive especially since it was proposed for the school of reserve officer and holder of a BTS Tourism level. Moreover, he noted that I was part of a family of 8 children and not 7 in reality. Furthermore, he pointed out that I had cut my wrists; however, to this day and despite fighting the disease for almost 20 years, I have no scars on my wrists. You may say that there was some confusion between the medical records, and no, I was not supposed to read his comments. Finally, you will not be surprised to know that the commander in question had just returned from Lebanon where he had seen the 88 victims of the Beirut attack on the French HQ. As a culmination, Commander Papeeta is said to have made a "tip of the iceberg" error that would have made him disavowed by his superiors; I have learned from unofficial sources that he is no longer a doctor.

For your information and with the support of those around me, I sent a letter to Mrs. Alliot Marie who forwarded it to the veterans in Fontenay sous bois. The retroactivity of pensions not being provided for in the pension code is the main reason for my request for intervention so that the harm suffered can be taken into consideration.
Please know that I will accept any medical expertise or appointment in your services in order to shed light on my atypical and singular path.
 I remain at your disposal and I ask you to receive, madam, sir, the expression of my respectful homage. Your devoted, IDOUAKRIM Abdallah Le beur-bère

Association of shit believing to defend minorities, I tore up their answer and finally told myself that if I could have had a copy of it you could have felt the same kind of reaction towards them. The cry I made at the time I gave them again and despite everything they do not accept to be a civil party defending me, History should not be written any more Than 7 or I do not know how many spears rather Six For silence On this world.

Charles Pasqua once said: "The freedom of individuals stops where the reason of State begins": This was practically my only contact with reality for a good ten years. The bad consideration after the incarceration in Egypt coming from the state was expressed when I needed a pass to bring my wife closer to me. In Rabat, And then shortly after the deposit of my collateral damage at Mrs AlliotMarie and then at the Veterans Affairs, I detect chemicals in my stairwell despite and even to the detriment of my daughters and neighbors, a suspicious gas causing irritation leading to eye infection and even skin infection, I seriously consider taking a photograph of my face to see the damage caused! Deliver him to me: During the incarceration, I sometimes heard voices, those of my family who were trying to comfort me during the ordeals I went through. This will be the first and last time, at least I am touching wood so that I don't have to relive this painful experience again. It has to be said that the use of cannabis accentuates these symptoms. Para-drowning: After a long period without treatment, one feels a sensation of extreme fullness bordering on bliss. At this point, despite the warning signs of deterioration, one no longer accepts criticism from relatives.

This period can be marked by a "bulimic" search for knowledge. And then, paranoia appears: a very difficult moment to manage. Sleep has practically disappeared and nights become longer and longer. When we ask ourselves questions about the Scanner and have the misfortune to open the "Quid", we read in the index: Scanner, Scanography, then "Scapa Flow" translated as "Escape, Take to the open sea". In fact, I learned from a nurse that it was a famous battle. However, paranoia set in, sustained by this strange coincidence.

 Anyway, following this fright, I will be torn by the desire to "take refuge" in Morocco. In fact, as far away as possible, which is like saying to my father's village in the Anti-Atlas. Enough to make even the most patient of doctors break down: The result of this trip was several years of effort on the part of Dr. Deddouche, who put a lot of effort into helping me stabilize myself. But, I repeat with a little bitterness, this trip was practically necessary to me as if I had received the order from Commander Papeeta to execute the leader of Hezbollah or I don't know from which faction. Is there a causal link between the disastrous experience in the French army and this journey to the same hotbed of tension that is the Middle East? I believe so. In fact, the events in France since the beginning of the second Intifada show that the Beur community identifies very much with the Palestinian cause. This reinforces my belief that if my trip had been publicized, even sponsored, I would not have been alone at the Rafaa border crossing. Since then I am supposed to be a "sleeper agent"; there was 9/11! ! ! I never slept, I growl at night in an unknown language.

Five years have passed since I left the feather and yet it had never really fallen silent. In an enlarged family context and always with the same woman in spite of reprehensible acts that will make me confess " For Mina ", For Mina,

Father, I wish this journey I wish to make could be prevented by a marriage to Mina. It was shortly before I left for Palestine. But you're insane, you've just had dinner with her companion. I was sad. Finally, and after a failed marriage with Chantal Barrière and especially my marriage certificate rendered void by court decision, I decided to return to Morocco to marry a woman my mother would have wished to be a virgin.

Mom, I've been married before and I can't accept a virgin girl. It was a stroke of fate that Mina recently got divorced, so I'm jumping at the chance to tell her the truth. It was on the bridge between Rabat and Salé that we were going to do our negotiations.
I tell her that I'm looking for a woman to guide me in religion; all she needs is a man who listens to her. However, while smoking with her brother, to whom I reveal my health problems temporarily masked by hashish, I think I am doing the right thing. After reaching an

agreement with Mina, we decided to set the date of the wedding with our parents, which was to be on the twenty-fifth of July, nineteen hundred and ninety-five. I still feel weakened by the treatment that I recently stopped, but I am exulting to marry a woman capable of running a household. I was aware of this when I saw her busy preparing cakes and dishes in the kitchen. After this famous wedding we go to Marrakech with our family and wait for family. I will always remember the complicity of my cousin's wife who passed me a bottle full of water to do our ablutions after the sex act; we were "just married" and my father's answer to a request for money so that my wife could go to the hairdresser: Shit on the children. After several visits to the French consulate, I was told that my marriage certificate, which had been invalidated, was insufficient and that I needed a birth certificate. I was administratively a bigamist. What always amazed me was why the omnipotent administration had not contacted the town hall of Montpellier where the civil registrar had not done his job. Six months passed with its share of happiness and misfortune. My wife had to undergo a fibromectomy and one of my cousins was a night lift to search the few dirhams that were in my pockets. All my fortune. I have the pleasant memory of having stopped smoking by running along the bridges between Rabat and Salé.

After much hesitation and an expired passport, I decided to return to Montpellier to meet the registrar. All it took was a phone call before I lost my temper and found myself monogamous in the face of French law. Fortunately, I send my corrected birth certificate in time. The mention of the first divorce is made in it. But in the "Mare Fétide" the wolves are on the lookout. I forgot to go see my doctor as my wife asked me, worse I indulge in drinking and hashish. Come celebrate your marriage, they should tell me. As my wife's arrival approaches, I decide to leave Palavas-les-Flots in Sète on foot; I will get there by night while losing consciousness.

Afterwards, I will be in the hospital's woozy atmosphere with a seismotherapy scheduled. At that moment only the wedding ring reminds me of my condition as a married man. I don't see anyone but the medical staff until the day when Mina, who had been waiting for me, enters the light at the door. Note the disappointment of the woman who thought she found her husband as she stepped off the boat. It should be remembered that the relationship between my mother and her daughter-in-law was tense: suspicion, perhaps even jealousy. The seismotherapy worked so well that I managed to get home from the hospital, but my mother will have a negative influence on my relationship because of the frequent fights. My wife will lose a fetus. I then decide to look for my own apartment. My wife can no longer bear to stay with her mother-in-law, so we spend weekends on leave at my brother's house in Fabrègues.

Mimoun will make me drink so much that I am unaware of the announcements he was making to my wife. The accommodation we will find will be a small F 2 that our beloved social worker, I quote Madame Demesterre, will help us to furnish. The only problem is that the apartment is cold with electric heating; we will save so much money that we will be given a substantial sum by EDF when we leave this first home for a more comfortable F3. My wife's efforts during this period are commendable; she passes the permit and works in an industrial fish shop. While seeking to give me a descendant. I can no longer count the number of IVF attempts aborted in pain for my wife. In the end, it is while going to see her uncle in Puteaux that the next period does not appear. I was about to become a father. As soon as I was late, I went to the pharmacy to get a test. POSITIVE At that time we had a Ford escort car that would soon be replaced by an Opel Astra after taking us to Morocco with our family for the first time. As far as I'm concerned, after several attempts, I passed the competition for reserved civil service jobs thanks to a typewriter lent by the Crdp. Its chief will also advise me to do a computer training course as I am entitled to under the employment solidarity contract.

This is a period when I regularly go after work to the library to see my classification in the official newspaper. I will end up finding myself well ranked for Paris, if my memories are good eighth. A move has to be prepared. After four months of pregnancy and my nomination for the dass de paris, we settle the formalities thanks to the CNC which will forward us our move and will take care of the furniture. A little before December 13, 1999, the date of my return to the administration, the move is completed.

After a move to Courbevoie, Imane's second birth occurs. But we won't stay there for long, I dream of a real estate project that will become a reality in Asnières-sur-Seine. The district is in the process of development but is still too lively in the pejorative sense of the term. I continue to smoke despite the huge bills of exchange. Seeing that I won't be able to get out of it, I call a real estate agent to sell the apartment. My parents good things will be there when he visits; we're not hiding anything anymore. After signing the promise of sale, I accept through the ministry the housing that will see me hit my wife. Indeed, I witnessed the stabbing of someone at the cotorep in Paris where I worked. The same evening I was screaming to the point of breaking furniture in my house. After having filed at the police station in relation to the aforementioned event, I was again in front of the police who advised me to calm down. Hate had set in and trust had worn out, according to my wife. I will touch her again the day she tells me that she no longer wants to make the trip to Egypt for fear that I will abandon her there. Hate had settled in. And then one day, tired of the Paris region and its greyness, I decided to go to Montpellier to see my family. She asks me for my keys for the next day's disinsectisation while her sister has them. Instead of calming down to say goodbye, I get carried away and hit her a third time. A mediation will follow !

KHASSARA / translate as "what a waste! "Tired of the warning shots of the ambient racism and in a (Soussi) concern to seek the truth or a truth, I came to construct the most obscure theories to explain this form of curse against the family. In the end, it is in the "split" not of Sylvius but of Abdallah that the reasons for my anger are to be found, and it is in a pseudo family tree that I go back to the beginning of the 16th century to find the presence of English people on Moroccan soil.

The death of the grandfather who fell into a well cannot be assimilated to a suicide which is a "haram" sin in the Muslim religion and I will not doubt the piety of this one "Allah y rahmou" may God give him thanks. I would like to stress here that falling into a well was one of the main causes of death at the time and I would not like to make this a crime of "lese family". One of the possible explanations would even be engraved in our name and that is why I am writing this part of the story, which is at least burlesque.

This is the story of Larsen IDOACREAM: English mercenary descended from a line of apothecaries, hence the name cream maker. I could really use it today. After the bitter defeat of the three monarchs near Ksar el Kebir, he found himself a prisoner of the Moroccan army. The European rulers again saw the threat of an Islamic reconquest over Spain and in a hidden desire to divert it, they sought to push the Moroccans back southwards "the Songhai and the Master of Gold". Thus they sent a troop of 3000 European soldiers and mercenaries led by Djouder Pacha to chew up the work of the Moroccans. The sentence of the prisoners of the battle of the three kings was commuted to incorporation into the expeditionary force. Thus Larsen returned to Marrakech in September 1590 almost free. On October 29, 1590, he left Marrakech with about 3000 other companions in search of fortune. In the vicinity of Taliouine, the troop settles for a stop near a village whose name I quoted in the first part of my manuscript. This is how the goal is reached; an ancestress could have been attacked by Larsen, which would support the thesis of the son of sin "ould el haram" but I will not be influenced by the easy solution dear to my wife's dictionary of insults. Larsen is rather beautiful and it is better to consider the seduction of a grandmother attracted by the blue of her eyes. He will nevertheless promise her to return after her mission and the transfer of her sentence. After days and days of walking, only a thousand of them arrived on the banks of the Niger on March 1, 1591. Their crossing of the Sahara lasted more than four months, much more than the fifty days of the Zagora sign. Their main asset is the possession of firearms which will give them superiority. It is at the battle of Tondibi, on March 12, 1591, that they will overcome the imposing army of Ishak II largely superior in number. The firearms will frighten the animals placed in front under cover, confirming the supremacy of the expeditionary force. Larsen will stain his hands with blood. The Songhaï army is routed at Tondibi and Larsen is chosen to return to announce it to the sultan. While most of the survivors will settle in, he will be left with another ordeal on his return with two other companions to announce victory to the sultan and the fulfillment of his promise. What he will do to find the one he discovered on his way. When he settles in Tamellakoute, he is asked to affirm his faith in the oneness of God and Mohamed his envoy, which he does without too much hesitation. The local Caïd will ask him his name which will be transcribed in IDOAKREAM; this thesis being pure fiction invented under the blows of the racists who saw in this name the allusion to a crime.

Besides, there is surely a statute of limitations for war crimes of this Larsen, but I tell myself that only divine punishment could explain any curse. At the employment agency, I was told I looked like a mobster when I applied for a job as a money courier by a counselor. I think it is necessary to recharge my batteries in this ancient part of the world (the tar is now less than 500 metres away) to ask the elders questions. So I plan to go there this summer. Maybe I could find the family tree there. My uncle is the elder kaid of the village. His son Abderrahman will succeed him after a well-deserved retirement. Would my ancestors have painted the frescoes of Tassili? This is my new thought after my return from Morocco. Indeed, I asked the family about the family tree. It turns out that my ancestors would have been among the first to settle in the region around the thirteenth or fourteenth century. Our origins would go back to a NASSER who came from Tata further south on the edge of the Sahara. Hence my suggestion that in older times the ancestors could have tagged the Tassili. On the other hand, making fictitious the story of the English mercenary Idoacream and reassuring me as to a doubtful origin and sin, the name of the IDOUAKRIM would have as a source an ABDELKRIM; to recapitulate, a NASSER coming from Tata then later a common strain in the Douar of my father the Iddaroubrahim, the Idelimame and the Idelharim. From my stay in Tamellakoute, I will keep the memory of having kept a will almost two centuries old referring to an older document.

Nineteen years of trying to piece together the past Snippets of a puzzle of words gone missing Take your medicine! It's just a vial. Take the medicine! Here they are laughing, To have destroyed everything in you, To the point where you want to live, But on a spring day, A letter arrives from the military archives denouncing the arbitrary power Of psychiatry as seen by Algiers, Which makes us shipwrecked! Primitive above all else, Thus expresses my disgust!

Serve
Submit
Acting
Isolated like that of Gir,
The survivor of the Atlas begins to roar
Healed on the Parnassus
Thanks to his faith,
He is finally upright again,
After almost dying more than once.

We like to cast shame, Especially xenophobic people, Because we find ourselves smarter, Than the vast majority of people! They make us the main cause of a society that implodes. The cause of their unhappiness Because they can't explain our happiness.

Like the snake on the caduceus, He inoculated me with the venom of thought, After taking the oath of a hypocrite When I needed the oath of Hippocrates His lies are his panacea Like those of the Algiers school! Should I have been called a "sucker" I had no shortage of boxes Why this corpse-like face? The answer is neuroleptic Haldol For this mad! decanoas injection Will kill this indomitable lion.

Under the pretext that the excuse of the death of conscripts has been tolerated by the government, I affirm that the military doctor whose path I crossed has practiced medical experiments on the patients he was supposed to cure,

 Would he have had complicity if not that of having been covered by Colonel Moutet, Or been seduced by the trips proposed by the laboratories or the incriminated laboratory or perhaps even an association of veterans having received donations from the said laboratory(ies).
In short, in almost two decades, one ends up doing one's own investigation when one has been the victim of arbitrary injustice. Abuse of power, my commanding officer or my colonel One day I even crossed paths with a gendarmerie colonel who, because I was supposed to have a helmet on a solex as a passenger, I recall, Well, this colonel put his P38 on my temple. That's what the French army was involved in,

Crusading for new people, at last since the Twin The way others look at the Muslim population is no longer the same. I anticipated that the invasion of Iraq would try to make a bridgehead for Iran, or even Syria, but we realize that the late Iraqi state will be dismembered by the neighboring powers, Iran should intervene to secure the holy places of Shiism such as Kerbala or Najaf after the departure of the Americans, the Kurds proclaim the independence of the Kurdish Republic and the Sunnis create the "Gaza Strip" of anti-Americanism from the ashes of Sunni power. Such could be the continuation of this part of the world, Historical Continuation Rather than Chaos.

I have been KNOCK OUT for almost 20 years of conflict with my state of asylum, Asylum seeker in a land of Freedom to seek medical attention, Equality - I end up adhering to the thesis in front of death, Brotherhood! with his family who is the only support in such situations, Splashed by all the miscellaneous facts of the brother's history. Who could finally be helped financially for the prejudice suffered

"My land is bleeding with a drop of blood! "On a bandage Gently laid on a white buttock Am I a bloody monster Or am I simply the most disgusting sleeper agent Agent who dreams of ghazalat in the Rif It's not an addictive delirium

But rather an emotional lack After so much overbearing behavior Why not short for a woman in the Rif?

She loves me that smokes kif If WE WERE STAR ENERGY LIKE STAR DUST STOP THIS Holly day

§§§ SANDY §§§

I met you in Cairo At the rise of a new generation These of Peace now

I thought I could be your hero (e) The " met " you were gathering in Cairo I gave you the cash to cure You invited me near the Nile to fat in Cairo I was may be so crazy To throw in the air an olive To receive it in my mouth And yours tried a lot to evict mine May be to intent not to love me Crossing the claim of Khan el Khalili Streets You were so sweet May be you're still alive I knew you when I hadn't the Khan dishes I was dealing in Cairo Eighteen-year's ago!

France, Legalise

it'll be less " Souss - France "

MAX the pit bull and FERAUD the Blair high,

I was born in the year of the Six Day War, At six years old In the year of the Yom Kippur War, I was lynched by Max the elementary school teacher Amateur boxing teacher who revels in the elementary One the war lasted six rounds Since then I blushed the wound Of the image of the Arab not sure

In high school, Féraud the badger used to throw me You're a virgin until I too became the lion to win my share of love.

I would like to take my leave Not to commit suicide But to escape to Morocco Dreaming of wanderings I had the idea To return to Salé With my father And in an emergency night I write this Reducing impact of Aldol On the vital energy of the individual Gandja or reduced zet Suffering As a counter-wave of vital energy less agitated Rebalancing all the psychic parameters Giving a sensation of pleasure in suffering I notice after an excess of thc A pain on the side Exactly at the place of the last injection My body is still-

PUB

Soul of Haldol

I'm struggling in my bed against the pain

My only happiness is to be in Morocco

After having tasted all the madness Why not stay in Salé
When I finally have some reason To stay at home My
daddy's reason Here I am there And "there" In Arabic
please
Commander Papeta was in the barracks exploded by
Hezbollah in 1982...
88 dead
Colonel Moutet who was above
crazy letter to Ang sang su khi
And the fatal silences of the Jihadist Or the one-legged
verbal Jihadist of France...

Ang Sang? You are under house arrest By the Burmese
junta I Abdallah Was assigned to insanity By France, a
democratic country By some officers Who kidnapped me
for twenty years Kidnapped the honey and the scene That's
all my sorrow

I can't help it, so Ang Sang Su Khi...

Do you see what France... Why a life with so much
suffering !!!!

Hospitalised in Laveran In the midst of the arbitrary Taken for a child And now I continue to take medication Intramuscular injection I think you think I blather Poor camel ! And yet A medicine As a bandage of the soul Poor donkey!

What about death in all this? And the wasted life of Mina! Who's got me what? Who gave me back the me! And my "We" "Hindu and Imanou" You gave me the "We" It wasn't a game I was in love and I still am every time I sleep I forget to think about our life back then. Kant ransacked by a gendarmerie colonel Who was fighting in the Algerian war In a small corner of Occitanie OCCITANIA

Ness janoub fi França Abdallah and the offence of facies Al ounsouria Result the caduceus Wa hanchou Li maadini Bi khatri Maa misquina The nurse Li kat dourb'haliya Hatta hiya Ma fahmach Aalech libra braha KAN BRIHA HIYA The nurse is beautiful Beautiful in her acts From the depths of my brain I associate the timeless image Of a shared burst of laughter Or of her smile placed In a drawer of my thoughts! Bend my soul! Do I say No I am alone Not near wings Of "them"? I don't have any, Zeal? Perhaps.

I would like to rewrite my first name Abd'Allah rather than Abdallah So that the fools and the unbelievers Return to God his capital letter At dusk I write Malik Oussekine He has made you mischievous too.

To supply remote areas Even if it were necessary to do so by using Diamond There this cheeky Neurologically

AND BECAUSE

I put on four skins to be "Handsome" I've always known it
Mental Hunchback
 Word lies Naked Moment not naked
Pretty sexually obsessed
 Since playboy And the other magazines I've received Re
suer To jerk off Sometimes to satiety in society In my
adolescence Since the silence The six spears of the tribune
Of the tribe of Oun Zine Who is mutely claiming The court
of Strasbourg For condemnation At least compensation for
the prejudice suffered I cannot be time-barred given the
circumstances This silence of 24 years of existence
Without substances Neuroleptic substances to break the
pain of the $alary Since Hallstatt I know it I even had to
split myself Sylvius' fissure

I would have split from Sylvie or Malika. Why not you,
Tanya? Mra Tania In Egypt fi al qahira Qalloulliya Mauri -
Tania

From the Moroccan I even consider the Algerian one.

See if she's as patriotic Or honest Rather than tipsy For that
France Ave maria des trompettes Ave maniac Papeeta

2,255th Thursday in my life How lucky I am! To survive it after so much slander Suffering broken by silence

Should I be that monster generated by Papeeta like Luke of George Lucas Waging war against Hezbollah Or the crusade like that Gilad who cried in gaza! I continue the fight As I said fi al Qahira

I can kill you with my pen!!!! Like I did in prison Adding a third eye To that poor bastard Who kept telling me over and over again i want to kill you He forgot that I was a thug I also avoided mass And even the officers' mess In the army Should I be alarmed I'm poorly armed You have to exhaust all recourses To get to court From a Bourg in the street STRASBOURG I NEED U THIS BOURG IN A STREET

Sabra I cry for you From Auschwitz to Chatila Same fight...

(Paris) - We had all dreamed so much of this South Africa, the symbol of a rainbow nation. We had been so joyfully moved on February 11, 1990 when we saw Madiba, the nickname given to Nelson Mandela in view of his tribe of origin, raise his fist in the company of his wife Winnie, from whom he had been separated for twenty-seven years! We had not been born on March 21, 1960 when sixty-nine people died from the bullets of the white apartheid police in Sharpeville. We had hoped so much when Madiba became the first black president of the Republic of South Africa and was sworn in on May 10, 1994 in Pretoria ...

Excerpt from an article on Google News
(Montpellier) - WE had all dreamed so much of this "Aqsa" Palestine, symbol of a radiant Islam. We had been so joyfully moved when we saw Abu Nasser, the nickname I give to Yasser ARAFAT in view of his victories against the Zionist occupier, shaking hands warmly and announcing the expiry of the PLO charter !!! To Ytzhaq RABIN this old demon and I say it to you tenderly during the chords that earned this valiant warrior death by his compatriot Perhaps a Zealot. We were born when the Christian militias and the army of Tsahal led by Ariel this other incubator of troubles as in Sabra and Chat Ila As when he massed the troops against the Arab part Sur al Aqsa Understand the esplanade of the mosques To better familiarize yourself With this history of Eternity

We had so hoped for when Abu Nasser became the first president of the Palestinian Authority in Ramallah...

For it represented all the hopes of having El Aqsa For me and all other Muslims Of all ages A place of pilgrimage No don't think of mirages Or stealth bombers I thought of that in this poem "Ariel Yasser and Houwa"

Sacred in the union Which of the two is the hawk more? When Ariel the old Palestinian Jew was talking to Yasser the young Bedouin he said to him one day Maybe even a yarmulke, "Now this is my land!!! "I'm sending you some for my treacherous plan to be written And for you your destiny as a stateless person saying: "You are no longer my brother! "However I keep your sister who could make me happy Fear that I will sweep away with a light breath Of Stealth Bomber please She will be my captive (captive Eve) of Eternity Like the city of light Where your dust will no longer rest! The Butterball for Yasser Arafat

I even like Mahmood wanted to burn the Bahruku Al Aqsa!

I dream of an Israeli-Palestinian confederation As I could dream of the Helveto-European It would bring wealth and prosperity to Israel as well as to Switzerland I have to think European on its four sides Israeli-Palestinian on its four times Of a song that makes peace grow greener In this first case Israeli-Palestinian Palestinian of yesteryear Singing of peace returned European on its 4 sides Kateb

chahid al Aqsa I could disappoint with losses and hassles Customs harassment I had some in Rafaa Military explanations Not in front of the general But in front of the commander in Laveran French military hospital My coming in these days Land saw Me before the arbitrary I wish my dream One day will come to an end And not me I am not king Old larva Old game madman I of chess and mate Where the "crazy" is queen In the arena Of the bullfighting That the cons cheering The advent Of war What a ringing But some laugh Bush, and even Tony The Butchery and the weapons turned to stone are raining Horse Butchery in times of famine Human this week The knights are buried The Arabian horse is exhausted See here these last words About what D'al Aqsa And what else? Allah y aatik l'kwa!!!! What a land for the beurbere.
When Occis denied you Choose your land to save this idea.

☐

THE FRENCH MOSSON @ Palestinian Jerusalem

For one US Moorish dollar

Palestinian, Philistine, Why Your People Don't Welcome Us At The Airport, Or Rafah Gaza's Strip The Streets of Gaza Should be like those of Al Qahira Cairo airport Medina's air port

Palestinian, You've got Death Sea I found Death Sea's Like suicide try That's my crime That's la "moisson française"

Palestinian, Can you tell me what's The Jewish "moisson" for you Injured children Death children Injured mother Death to the elder That's the Israeli productions Come to BALL (y) country Making joy In the neck of the Palestinian'state, We 'll make it a war film for the children Should say George to his child Since thousands of Palestinians Are imprisoned, Injured, KILLED FOR A DOLLAR Maure.

Elephant People

You've got Dead Sea But "the beurbère"
Found Death seas S U I C I D E That's the French production

In the nineteenth century The society des nations turned Your name into a new theft, Stealing your Antiquity May be also paternity P A T R Y

Mahmood it's TOO LATE For me to say to you That your letters are our falling Falling but hoping One day,

Israeli'LD build airport Inside this scaring "wall" closing Everyone who wants peace Supposing defend Them!

Tzipi, You can improve life of a new trend, Life of people Who try to forget war! A new pilgrimage route Would provide a new source Of incoming to this poor country. Al Qod's pilgrimage What I was always dreaming about. Its now to late for a suicide for the Patria !!! I claim this right to see you yourself The Palestinian or rather Philistine Since my destiny was fulfilled By the coming not of the rain The rain of existence The support of existence Angels To the angel Or the war of my 20 years

The war of a good Twenty hatred of years Below France To seek the deal A To reassure myself in the breasts of French women Within French society It is Mina the Moroccan woman Who knew how to change my hate In love It is Mina Who m gave in exchange Two years I

To my angels Hind and Imane

The war of a good Twenty hatred of years Below France To seek the deal A To reassure myself in the breasts of French women Within French society It is Mina the Moroccan woman Who knew how to change my hate In love It is Mina Who m gave in exchange Two years I

To my angels Hind and Imane

OFFICIAL DEALER VERBS

V (h) Official BERBER ERBES

In Poitiers La Kabila Martel Hammered us In Montpellier The Blackfoot broke my feet At the Garrigues camp then at Laveran (Marseille) The commanders Injected Psychotropic drugs I stop there !!! Ooh La La ? My war of twenty years As my face Does not interest anyone Except maybe you You my children 20 years of war Against the arbitrariness Of Freemasonry Me son of mason Who participated in the construction of this Nation

A perfect civil servant Thanks to the dispensary The soldiers wanted to silence this feather That lights The bottom of the most secret thoughts Those that the neuron secretes

Ya ayouri, ya tafounaght!

Laughs Hind Do not idolize me Imane I ask you to forgive I have not left your mother I never wanted to displease you Refrain Imane They inject the salt of pain To your father this misfortune Happy I am by you I do not forget you or pruacakakaka Hind chorus, Coffee table I do cross-pain Yesterday in front of a pint Today writing my lament Composed of bitter worms Chorus So literary verses For the moons of my heart Proud hearts Maybe because of mother Left alone in misfortune Refrain Separated hearts Choir torn apart I hope you feel That I make blood Nine of my writings

Oh mum
Oh my moon
Oh my sun

YOU are not in the Louvres!!!

You're not in the Louvre When you've been to prison You don't even care to wear mink Or even Kashmir When you've been to prison You're not stupid to make sure you have a lost reason When you've been to prison No matter what, At the door It's rarely a buddy Who opens the door You're not in the Louvres Nanterre prefecture For roofing Nanterre university For home Nanterre city For the vile girl Homeless Sure to party And get your head broken In the streets Lost Only your steps in the Louvres make me forget these heavy trials.

In HIND and IMANE (it's their footsteps)

KHEYRA KHTARTILIYA SOFA Cashmere FI BLAD
L'H MIR Fi bilad al ahram MISRa Brazil de meu corazao

BETTINA

AGORA DJEMBE Now I love bé I love Bettina I could
say Without thinking of harming myself I kept this picture
Where you showed yourself holding a coconut To make
dream this bird Of the islands Who desires My BETTINA
I would have wished for children of you Under my straw
roof Before my funeral!

EL BEIJAFLOR DE AMOR Tu passaro silente

*AN ANSWER TO THOSE QUESTIONS? WHY
SADDAM DIED? HOW ANTIC MENS CAME TO
WATER? Like you and me everyday in our shower !!!
AND THE BEST WHY THERE'S NO DOUBT ON IT A
PROBLEM BETWEEN THE MOSLEMS AREA AND
WESTERN COUNTRIES ?*

The MEN, This big-foot fallen on water, The first Adam
and Eve's must have escaped from the terrific smilodons
crossing rivers swimming, From savannas to Rift Valley,

Lucie and Companions Must have sung " cross the pool at your leisure, Dame Lucie and I the Berber I'll crawl by yourside Speaking in an ununderstood language like mine Without the sense of Cartesianism my high school teacher told me.

Moreover, shortly afterwards, no longer in high school but between the Paleolithic and the Neolithic, there were hydraulic civilizations (Egyptians, Greeks or Mesopotamians testify to this) and Arabs building boats "outloubi l ilm oualaou fi Sinn". And in China you have to get there thanks to a good monsoon and good instruments and the best maps of the moment. On other shores we discover the Americas maybe with young adventurers as I could always be in search of a new light of a different "elsewhere".

DO THE LATINOS HAVE BERBER BLOOD ON THEIRS? do the south americans have berber blood on theirs? Los latinos tienen sangre berber? Pienso que tenemos que comparar la sangre de estos pueblos. I'd be in favor of a hematological survey of these populations. It's a hypothesis Es una hypotésis pero

Long life to Chavez, Lula and Evo Morales ! ! !

During history there are three at least possible reasons to hate Occidental countries

And in the other side make war by eleventh September dan Crusade linked to the owning or harbours in the holy land grocery terminal on the eastern Mediterranean with its share of atrocities committed by the Franks (acts of cannibalism in Maari)

But also acts of enrichment that made the Templars' treasure.

So we say Crusades, spices and in the nineteenth century when America emerged the oil from which it wanted to immerse itself with on the one hand the enrichment and on the other hand the crumbs given to the ruling class to kill the snake in the egg !!! The CIA has already destabilized an Iranian minister long before the oil shock of the seventies And finally, one of the main reasons's why Saddam was killed Is that he nationalized Iraqi's petroleum!

He DIED BECAUSE HE DID ALLAH AKBAR

DCDH SWORD WAR

Dreams of Oc

In the past and as a sleeper agent I did not have France condemned at the time I have always reserved myself as my job with the Ddass at another time I return to the Pays d'Oc it dreamed me 'Oc

the commission of the veterans in the 94 that reminds me of a tax rate l' Oc high Fabrègues What am I looking for? bricks of the real ones and a villa for the fada a world tour for which I win it in line no c' Oc aîne lines of writings on my deconfigured mine would say Lafayette.

Wars and farts

here is the Russian translation of tolstoy made "war and peace" which is antinomic

From: Sonia Bois Sent: Monday, March 12, 2012 6:23 PM To: abdallah idouakrim Subject: Re: FW: VICTIMS OR NOT OF THE COMMANDER PAPEETA
 I was programmed to shoot Nasr'Allah that is why I made the incomprehensible trip to Gaza to sympathize with the Al aqsa Martyrs Brigade and then ask to return home through the strait the phosphorus bomb had injected me so invective I had to burn not as I said el Aqsa in a poem inspired by the act of this

Australian or this Israeli soldier for Hardened Lead wars no longer have the name of wars hardened lead restore Hope c 1 message my message c that I need a massage a jacuzzi a yakusa I am Who makes capoeira! at 45 years old minus 25 YEARS OF MENTAL PRISON Others say political asylum where ? a French Arab immole Sheikh Nasr'Allah in Lebanon with a phosphorus bomb naturally I can no longer go to Morocco by following the advice of this unbeliever a to bring down Nasr'Allah that's why I made the incomprehensible journey to Gaza.

sympathize with the Al Aqsa Martyrs Brigade then ask to go home through the strait the phosphorus bomb had injected me so invective I had to burn not as I said el Aqsa in an inspired poem by the act of this Australian or this Israeli soldier for Hardened Lead the wars no longer have the name of wars hardened lead restore Hope c 1 message my message c that I need a massage a jacuzzi a yakusa I am Who makes capoeira! at 45 years old minus 25 YEARS OF MENTAL PRISON Others say political asylum where ? a French Arab immole Sheikh Nasr'Allah in Lebanon with a phosphorus bomb naturally I can no longer go to Morocco by following the advice of this unbeliever

to kill Nasr'Allah that's why I made the incomprehensible trip to Gaza to sympathize with the Al Aqsa Martyrs Brigade and then ask to return home through the strait the phosphorus bomb had injected me then invective I had to burn no not as I said el Aqsa in a poem inspired by the act of this Australian or this Israeli soldier for hardened lead wars no longer have the name of wars hardened lead restore Hope c 1 message my message c that I need a massage a jacuzzi a yakusa I am Who makes capoeira! at 45 years old minus 25 YEARS OF MENTAL PRISON Others say political asylum where ? a French Arab immole Sheikh Nasr'Allah in Lebanon with a phosphorus bomb naturally I can no longer go to Morocco by following the advice of this unbeliever

Is Rael

Your land is beautiful Raï Bar reintroduces evening primrose The wild soul, the ostrich But you cheat with the philistines You saved the Nubian ibex Will you save the Palestinian? On you, Lipzy, depends the survival and the destiny of the philistine; The Khouïa reserve, The Gaza Strip, The Gulf of Aqaba Yaël, You save the high bodies Shaï Shafir Who plunges me into the caressed dream Of swimming with dolphins of Eilat But it's too late Jews I'm not hating you! Jude let me love you! Save Palestine In the garden of the 7 plants The pomegranate that exposes itself And explodes only in my taste buds; The vine, the olive tree, the wheat, the barley and the fig As a taste of Eden Naga, Don't you think you're Süleyman In fact I'm Salah ed-Dinn Freeing el Aqsa not as a king My only weapon is the mouse and the feather I want the land where milk and honey flow From the dates of Jericho As a date I'd like the end of chaos! From the Naqba that endures Right of Zion goes hand in hand with the right to return If you love your neighbor Be friends and like Sadat Be faithful to your words That fly away in funny bursts Of drones : It's still funny This role-playing game because like Gilad I'll take the legion of honor On el Aqsa for Sabra and the sabiaa Of war I don't want The human pressure will disappear Forget the Naqba Sheikh Yacin will congratulate you And Hamas will disarm As u keep quite and safe biblical animals Let biblical people safe and free For a safer Palestine.

Your fate

"Let's get out of the nuclear age! Let's get out of the Chemical Age! "Says the Butterball, Poor Wanderer Wanders Classic He knows we're slow To secure all the reactors To plug all the exhaust pipes He doesn't lie Because he's a dad He thinks about the thousands of years that nuclear waste has been rotting away at life

Anti-Chernobyl Anti-Fukushima Which one next It's the deal Daddy don't deal Don't deal Tell them Daddy Never again Fuku Might as well take fugu Never again Chernobyl That's my deal Otherwise why not deal?, Why not kill? Like that Gilad who gets the Legion of Honor for killing the Palestinian taken for a dog.

Let's enter the ecological era. And our geostrategic area will become a new America thanks to technology.

I therefore affirmed: "all the solutions exist, micro-enterprises with little help can perhaps one day help Humanity. "Since Adam descended from Eden in the Holy Land with Eve, they have between them two IN LOVE, they swarmed not in arbitrary; their children Cain and Abel killed each other This is indeed the original sin Started again Their descendants then dispersed From the Middle East To Africa, the Far East And later Europe And then the Americas Where was born the new order? From the capital This executioner From the capitals Of the whole world And especially from the Third World. »

Ah ibad' Allah or Cervantes

Why did Don Quixote fight against windmills and why was there an inquisition after the Reconquista?

don fought against windmills because he rejected the pigs of the Muslim world like the windmills introduced into Spain by the Arabs!

Shortly after the Reconquista there was the inquisition because this first in the history of Europe had an important setback : the admiration of the then uncultured Christians for the marvels of technology (astrolabe at the head) of Islam Christopher Columbus passed through the pig of Tangier where he was in contact with Muslim (I'm not going to be a revisionist) and Jewish sailors.
There was an important wave of conversion due to the mixing of populace and the inquisition had to stop everything! The war was won but the war of ideas was lost da "vinci" pardon I say in advance. I WRITE IN MINUSCULE thank you for your attention for a message not written at dusk but at dawn I love this poem I love it I hope you too if I write like that It is that "ça va pas!" followed shrink for a little more than twenty years at 20 YEARS I was a child

Now I am waiting for the death of the Moor who is writing to you right now is what you like to read me is what you like to hear me say that the commander "Papeeta" has been relentlessly fighting for me in this early spring of 1988 5 years ago for him after his return a young beurbère beur and berber at the same time and in faith I have faith to be finally recognized not as a paratrooper dead in combat but as ".... COLLATERAL DAMAGE OF THE HEZBOLLAH BY PAPEETA" and finally the granting of at least ONE SYMBOLIC EUROS FROM THE REPUBLIC I AM PASSING ON THE OTHER SIDE OF THE MIRROR I'm going to drown my sorrow in my bathtub can being an ante-mortem message after going into intensive care just about three years ago YES THE REPUBLIC made me PSYCHOTIC I AM IN NEUROLEPTICAL SUBSTANCES FOR LACK OF NEUROLEPTIC SUBSTANCES IT SAID : Haldol for this madman he took me for a crazy faggot it was in the fatal medical file I still write to you without desire of Moorish or death I am of Berber origin born at the commissioner's by moving from the police station avenue du professeur GRASSET the old maternity here in Montpellier 45 YEARS ago NOW THAT I AM AND WHO AM I? A FORMER MEMBER OF THE DASS DE PARIS WHO SERVED AT THE GARRIGUES CAMP IN DECEMBER 1987

MY FIGHT EL AQSA

I said COLLATERAL DEGAT OF HEZBOLLAH AND I REMEMBER NASRALLAH I was in 1989 in RAFAA just after a trip to Brazil in Salvador de Bahia which saved my life ! after the disastrous military experience I drink alcohol and disintegrate with Haldol by regular injections every 3 OR 4 WEEKS PLEASE CONTACT MY DOCTOR DRAGONNU (pronounces or) TO KNOW IF I AM A FOUNDATIONALIST assassiyoune in the language of Voltaire I have not committed any crimes the only thing is to call me IDOUAKRIM I'm not making it up, it's my family name, I join the family of the paras who died for France. I almost did since this abusive internment, abuse of the exclusive power of the French army, "the Great Mute", is constantly being repeated but can- Be that I psychosis OWN NO MEDICINES But rather MEDICINES OR LIKE

ALL OTHER DISABILITIES AN AAH A TELEVISED ADDRESS TO ME TO EXPLAIN ME ABOUT ALL THE MISSED ATTACKS I MAY CLAIM! I AM PACIFISTE I PROPOSE The establishment of a UN status for the AQSA AT LEAST the rest is left to them I must be reactivated during the 7th Arab-Israeli war I took some durable rabe in my passage to the army beating for learning of life at the time when everyone was leaving zen in the club dancing, I didn't do any of this I was not there monumental mental death here is my story of a tribune who seeks the tribune of the court to raise a tribute for his tribe   and   his   people!   !   !
llllllllllllllllllllllllllllllllllllllllllllllllllllllllllllllllllllllllllllllllllll
lllllllllllllllllllllllllllllllllllllllllllllllllllllllllllllllllllllllllll
lllllllllllllllllllllllllllllllllllllllllllllllllllllllllllllllllllllllllllllllllllll

lllllllllllllllllllllllllllllllllllllllllllllllllllllllllllllllllllllllllllllllllllllllll
lllllllllllllllllllllllllllllllllllllllllllllllllllllllllllllllllllllllllllllllllllllllll
lllllllllllllllllllllllllllllllllllllllllllllllllllllllllllllllllllllllllllllllllllllllll
lllllllllllllllllllllllllllllllllllllllllllllllllllllllllllllllllllllllllllllllllllllllll
lllllllllllllllllll! ! ! De escribir las noches Sin dormir durante
dias
Solo unas horas

AUTHOR'S BIO

02/02/1967 Birth at the maternity hospital in Montpellier,
year of the Six Day War.

 Childhood in Cournonterral shared between the local
school, the garrigue and the river (Coulazou).

18/03/1973 Birth of the little brother (who lent his photo
on "collateral damage from Hezbollah") Rachid and the
Yom Kippur war. Following the oil shock, we are
considered as scapegoats for the expensive life.

10/1977 Arrival at La Paillade (future Mosson) and schooling up to BTS Tourism option welcome in 1987 Death of Malik Oussekine and first demonstration; in December, I anticipate the call and here I am at the 3rd RI of pièmont at the Camps des Garrigues.

1988 Definitive reform at the HIA Lavéran by Colonel Moutet and Major Papeeta, a psychiatrist noting lacerations on my wrists that I still do not have at the age of fifty. No need for a scan to support his contradictions because he had survived the Drakkar attack a few years earlier and had a big grudge against Muslims.

The neurologist brother-in-law employs me as a driver.

02/02/1989 1st trip to the unknown and boarding on an inaugural flight of el Condor; Paris-Fortaleza with champagne. 21 years old and Brazil from the favelas to the 5 stars ($200 in pocket and the silent bird discovers himself a different lover).

1989 More politically and civilly involved trip: my green march to Jerusalem. 1990 Cairo and the American University Library. "Entry denied" in Rafaa: the soiled passport will be purified by fire at the oxford boarding house near Tahrir Square. Incarceration: I am like pharaoh dead in the mastaba reminds me of the newspaper "al ahram".

24/04/2000 Birth of my daughter Hind 03/12/2001 Imane 2007 Year of divorce and descent into hell.

2013 Marriage with Asmae of whom I like to say: you amuse me; you are my muse 24/11/2014 Arrival in France of Asmae. 15/09/2017 Birth of Salah our son.

Clarification:

i FOMBEC: Acronym recalling the principles of good camouflage: F of substance, shape, Shadow, Movement, Noise, Radiance, Color. ii VSL: Voluntary Service Long (18 months at the time) iii GI's: American Soldiers iv Piranha: refers to Brazilian street girls (not all of them are prostitutes). v Ibad-Llah: Plural of Abdallah. vi Zabt: Policeman

Acknowledgements :

I would like to thank all those who will get there without being too weary Of my linguistic interlacing. At this moment, I think of all those without whom the adventure would not have been possible, from my family in Morocco to the anonymous people who have had a special look at me.

www.ingramcontent.com/pod-product-compliance
Lightning Source LLC
LaVergne TN
LVHW041738190726
843493LV00008B/2417